Head Work

Jonathan S Baker

Dearest Reader,

This project for me began years ago. Unfortunately, I only began working in earnest a few months ago. I was someone who wanted to be a writer but didn't write. I have a history of doing that, not doing things. I've wanted to be a friend but wasn't, wanted to be a lover and wouldn't let myself. It took me hurting someone for a long time to realize that I needed to change. Before I tried changing though I went out and found other people to hurt. This work to me represents a pretty big change in myself. It may not be evident in the poems to follow, but I think I'm a better person, writer, friend, and lover. As you read these think about what you want to be. If that is already you congratulations. Otherwise, try asking yourself why you aren't there yet. Don't beat yourself up over it. Just address recognize it, address it, and move on. If you fail, then try again.

Sincerely,

Jonathan S Baker

In the Therapist's Office

Wispy strings of sage filled that place
I winced as the gaunt old man
scraped the sharpened bone blade
across the wood tray
separating the hen into neat sections.
If you're ever in that strange port
it only costs you your comfort
and the price of a bird
to hear his words
and gain insight into the pathway
that leads to your own wishes.
He drives his fingers deep
into the bloody organ matter
making the clouds that hide
the future to scatter
and he bends his ears to the center
of universe where we all started
and hopefully he finds
your purpose there
and you find that you're not
too far off the course.
He will shine an old paper lamp
towards your goals and the obstacles
that you keep.
If you are lucky
you will only weep.
a little bit.

Mental Masturbation
with an Audience of One

First of all,
if you're not in therapy
you should go.
It's some of the most
gratifying self pleasure
I've ever experienced.

"I don't think you're a narcissist."
I don't know, maybe you're right.
You've got the learning
but I'll tell you this I'm so self-absorbed
that just the suggestion of narcissism
makes me fold in on myself like
a self reflective ouroboros
and puts me in a feed back loop

"I don't think you're manipulative."
Well thanks, Chad, I mean that,
but I may have only told you
the parts that I knew would
get you to say that.
Two reasons
first off I need people,
even you, to like me,
and secondly and more importantly
I don't want you
to jam my shit up for 72 hours
and I don't want to re-lace my shoes
so I may have given you
a dry toast and water version
of my point of view.
Anyway if just the inconvenience of egress

is enough to get me through the night
then I probably okay, right?

"I don't think you're a monster."
Well again thanks,
but you kind of took my best excuse away.
If I was a monster though
I' d probably be one of those
retro future robots
from one of those old
black and white sci-fi shows
and I could be defeated
when I couldn't compute
real human emotion.

Dear Everyone I Know

What I really meant
when I said "Hey"
was I missed you
earlier today
and I was hoping
there was someway
we could be
in the same place
at the same time
without running away.
I hope you know this

Meadowlark

Everyone should have a time
when things go just so right.
The path to the hoop is so clear
that you can just barely hear
way off in the background
the jaunty whistle of
Sweet Georgia Brown.
Every man, woman, and child
dunking on that punk life
with the crowd going wild.

Everyday Heroes

The closest some will be
to the championship belt,
the cup, the trophy, or ring
to being the king or the queen
of all creation, everything
is a job done right
followed by a restful night.
They win no cheers of fans
or start riots in the stands,
but way back behind
that mask that hides
their wants and needs,
their hopes and dreams
is a high power drive
fueled by gallons
combustible of pride.

Set the Timer 15 min.

Breath in and out.
Continue and repeat.
Release the world.
It will release you.
Now it's just you,
your mind and body
in the darkness.
Your body is filling
with your being.
Like warm water
poured into the container
that is you and taking
the shape of you.
You haven't felt
this way in forever.
Your mind can't even remember
the last time you were aware
of your own body.
Your body remembers.
Inside the banks of every cell
is the recorded history of you.
Flow back to that moment,
traveler, future man.
Slide back to that time
when you decided
not to feel anything
ever again.
Fall back to when
numbness became
preferable to life.
Go all the way
back to the womb
if you have to.

Traveling as synaptic pulses
a brilliant blue ball
of love and light.
Be there and be
the angel of mercy
appearing before
a button sized clump that one day
will be the being that is you.

Give unto that life,
that not quite yet
human thing,
a lesson of love.
Let yourself know
that you will make
it at least this far
and even farther.
Let him know
you've traveled
through space
over 940 million miles
every year for decades.
You've traveled
through time
farther than all
those who quit
or didn't make it.
Let that ball know
that it will be
up to the challenge.
Scraped knees, broken bones,
great loves, great heartache,
and he is going to keep
going back for more.
Right back up on the horse.
Give your loving lights a flash

and snap back, return.
Return to now.
Still feeling yourself,
remembering yourself
from both perspectives
you as the traveler
seeing your protoplasmic form
and you as that clump of cells
being reaffirmed.

a moment in time

just a point on the line

the line that runs forever back
into the misremembered past
and forward into the unwritten future

Close your eyes tight
now count to nothing

This is what it feels like

Now live in that place

repeat ad infinitum

that is our eternal space

(the only thing that matters)
NOW
←   !   →
before   after
(doesn't mater)   *(doesn't matter)*

Roadblocks

"Life isn't fair."
Bullshit!
Life, the world, the system
isn't some uncontrollable force
like an earthquake or a hurricane.
Life is people
who have the capacity
to behave in a fair manner.
Life is made up of choices
and reactions.
Life is how you respond
to uncontrollable forces.

"It is what it is."
This is another way
that midlevel micro managers say
"Hey I gave up
and you should too."
It's another way
to acknowledge
that a problem exists
and you are not
only going to do nothing
but you're going to stand
in the way of change.

"You got to do, what you got to do."
Well fuck your plans
and shove your schemes!
What I got to do
is work on my goals
and follow my dreams.

DIY Shame Box Removal

Your Parents, teachers,
and youth group leaders
built you a box of pain
and they did it out of love
and a misguided attempt
to keep you safe and sane,
but it has never been a good fit.
It makes you slouch a bit.
It Inhibits your view
and it numbs you
to love and joy
and the kind of pain
that makes us want
to try again.

Step 1:
Feel your feelings.
This part is messy
and my leave you reeling.
Some of those things
may have spoiled
over the many years
so find a well ventilated place
and a loving friend
to hold your space.

Step 2:
Share your feelings.
This part might hurt.
Who am I kidding?
It will most definitely hurt
You will ache
Just remember,
anger and hate

those are just masked
sadness and fear,
and that crying you hear
that's just you
getting through.

Maslow's Lament

What are the differences
between your wants and your needs?
Though on the face they really must seem
as near each other as the number two is to three,
but there is in fact a divide
as vast and frighteningly wide
as a red rock ravine,
but is joined by a bridge
that spans in between.
Like the days Monday and Sunday
together are squeezed
but in reality are kept parted
by the rest of the week.
To confuse or to switch them
can lead to your doom.
Like comparing a mist
to a downing monsoon.
You may want for riches, comforts, or wealth
but needs must be fulfilled for the sake of your health.
So, know that I have considered all of the above
when I claim my greatest need to be only love.

Lost in the weeds
or How to Succeed

Set up, research,
Starting out
find a quiet place,
a place
that moves you
and inspires you.

Find an area
free of distractions,
a comfortable spot.
A park is nice
or a cemetery
If you need
Wi-Fi or a plug in,
try a café
or the library.
If it fits your schedule.

Having a plant
nearby is nice.
What kind of plant?
Should it be a succulent
or maybe fern?
Have a drink handy
Hot coffee, tea iced
or a warming
and soothing
liqueur.
Just enough to lube the flow.

Choose your tools.
Work in pen.
It's like working

without a safety net.
Work in pencil.
Keep a mistake
from being a regret.
Use the computer
It's the year two thousand
and something
Catch up.

Set your margins.
Choose your fonts.
Adjust your chair.
Clean your desk.
Move the fern.
Water the fern.
Research fern care.
Refill your coffee.
Spill your coffee.
Get a towel.
Sit back down.
Stare at the screen.
Look at the time.
Hours have past.
Good work.
You're all ready
for next time.
Congratulate self.

Training the Words

The words taunt
float just beyond reach
not yet ordered and purposed.
They test me.
They spin and dance,
dogs desiring attention,
unable to convey their needs.
The words bark in the mind
meaninglessly and endlessly.
If in a frustrated rage,
I coerce them, push them
force them onto the page,
they form blurred words
dictated by a liar
and inked by a fool.
I need to guide them
gently and lovingly
the words to the page
and find their place.

Sabotage thy Self

Ah gee,
I mean really?
What if I become
more complete
as a person,
ya know?
Like, what if
I become more
more tolerant
and more accepting,
and I get over myself
my habits, my hang ups,
and my own shames,
and everyone else
stays the same old same?

Come on,
think about it.
What if I really think
and meditate
and I get enlightened
and learn and create
and share
only to find that
no one really cares?
I could end up being
a totally different guy,
like a dependable person
that loves fearlessly
without conditions,
but I mean, shit,
what if I become
a better person
all for nothing?

BFF

Awash in ember blaze
of the end of days
the enthralled crowd
stood mesmerized
slack jawed awaiting
final judgement,
but we two friends
felt no fear or shame.
We worried not
whether Hell or Heaven
called our names.
Our world existed
in those few moments
for all of forever.
We were in it together,
this damnation.
I crack a defiant grin.
As Gabriel's Horn blows
and the seas boil
beasts rampage and
the dead come home,
you pull out your phone.
Laughing at yourself
as you would always,
and you say
"Let's take a selfie."

Seating Charts

"Red Rover, Red Rover,
send Johnny on over!"
Back when we was kids,
Abrams, Barret, Clements,
the ABCs chose our friends.
It was simpler then
when seating charts
protected our hearts.
I miss not feeling defeat
as I look for a seat
for a place just to eat.

But I'm all grown now
and can't remember how
oh just how it was done
to just let go and
to just have fun
with whoever or
with just anyone.

Letter Service

Everyday
I drop off bad news
stick people with bills,
deliver packages
meant to fill the holes
in peoples lives.

A lot of time to think
to talk to myself
to mull over past decisions
letting the locusts sing
in my ears.

A lot of time to wonder
about the women I know
and the ones I don't
and how they're the same.

A lot of time to let
the sun blind me
or the rain wash me
or the wind go through me.

A lot of time to imagine
the people behind those doors
receiving hate mail, love letters,
and threats and scams.

A lot of time to compare
myself to them
to see where I stack up
against the faceless
only names and numbers.
A lot of time

Being Human Again

My jumpstarted heart
all scar tissue and rot
aches.

From each unwilling donor
I've gathered lifetimes of loss.
A corpse's reanimated anxieties
race through this
second hand mind
terrorizing it a second time.

Countless strangers' regrets
furrow this stitched brow.
Chance after chance
for love
slipped from these
ill gotten hands.

My body burns
to be caressed again
by a woman
I never knew.

My legs yearn
to take me to a her
I never met.

My guts churn.
I carry the guilt
of a dozen long dead men
each holding on to mistakes
I never made.

Victor's greatest sin
was never playing God,
but making a man
to live these pains again.

Teratoma

Flesh shaped and molded
to Cronenberg's ideal
twisted malformed
constant companion
smiling jagged
just a bit of bone
and a patch of hair
a lump of biting clay
painful little sprite
mongrel cells
fighting filthy dirty
going straight for
the soft bits

Familiar Strangers

The extras, the people
we see but never meet,
or we meet but never know.
The burner folks
existing on the fringes
of our routines.
Women, like the street singer,
that you mean to tip
but she is always on
the opposite corner.
Men like William Clindor
who is no more
than a name printed
on an insurance mailer.
Existing like a phantom extremity,
like a vapor in the purgatory
of our periphery.
All are guilty
of avoiding the risk
the chance jarring
of our routines
by extending a small bit
of human affection
to salvage unrealized connections
never extending a hand to hoist
these strange beautiful creatures
into our own world.

In The Waiting Room

When the hospital bed arrived
cold metal and sanitary
with sheets like sandpaper.
The living room wasn't that anymore.
Bed pan, pressure cuff,
a rarely used walker,
needles, pill bottles,
all the clutter of cancer.
No one there was truly alive.
Living had become waiting.
Waiting for shots and doses
and trying and failing
to convince her to move
for her own sake.
It was a preemptive wake.
Waiting for the diseased
to become the deceased.
Waiting for something
to do or to say.
Waiting for a better day
and feeling the guilty and dirty
for thinking that way.

Suffering someone's pain.
Suffering through their shame.
Suffering through time and boredom.
Listening to the prayers
and hollow choruses
of visitors' platitudes
those old familiar tunes.
Keep your chin up
through Jesus all things,

and on and on, etc.
Sitting there sulking and angry
and knowing that
you are a horrible person
because one day this
will be over for you
and the hospital bed
will one day be removed.

Fun Factoids about the Human Body

Did you know
that your nose
can remember
thousands of scents?
Locked away
inside of you
is the memory
of the smells
of your first meal
away from home,
the smell of the
girl who first
kissed your cheek
but also the reek
of mom's vomit
during chemo.

Did you know
that a baby
starts life with
about sixty
more bones
than an adult?
You lose much
along the way.
Time, memories,
friends, and family.
They're not really
gone though.
The bones fused
as stronger pieces,
just as the rest
of your life

has fused into you.

How about this?
There are over
a hundred thousand miles
of veins carrying blood
through your body?
Most people will travel
less through their life
than their own blood cells,
but the iron in our blood
and the calcium in our bones
come from ancient explosions
of giant stars,
and we stand
locked on Earth
stranded in these
human bodies.

A Look Back at Some of the Women I've Loved and Their Vaginas
in no certain order

B. was a welcome mat
a well worn catcher's mitt
tanned and oiled to perfection.

J. full of lies,
T. full of sadness,
C. full and fun.

L. a warm, inviting place
a turbulent river of love
and robust wine.

S. a mixture of moscato
and electricity.

Beautiful Confusion

Everyday, every breath,
every long conversation
brings the new.
New virtues, new vices,
new hopes, new rules,
new possibilities, new chances.
An entire universe
created or destroyed
on the whims of lovers.
The old reshaped and changed.
What comes next is unknowable.
With wanton disregard
for everything safe and stable.
Tomorrow's poetic moment
is yesterday's unformed fantasy.
Open up your heart box
and dump it all in.
Your beliefs and thoughts,
your joys and griefs.
Place your bets with the staff.
The crank turns. Bright lights burn.
Your life tumbles into new
fantastic formations.
Will you hear that satisfying
jackpot ring?
Or, will you lose the lot
and wish you could take it all back?

Aimless Wandering

When I fail to plan
a driving schedule,
a proper route,
a specific destination,
or any rest stops
along the way,
I'm sorry.

Understand, Love,
that my only goal
is to travel along with you
and as long as we
share this life
things are going
according to my plan.

She searches the land
Her eyes look to the sky
Her soul is found there

The Empty Patch

Down the street is a vacant lot
unused, abandoned, idle, untended.
The rain water and all the filthy runoff
collects in the valley of a clogged storm drain
and fills most of that square of neglected earth.
A lone tree with twisted and gnarled branches
stands in the corner by the broken and worn stone
foundation of a now long gone home.
The noncontiguous grass stands knee high in places
hiding snap ankle holes and jags.
In general it is a blight to the neighborhood.
With the right perspective and the right light
in that spot between day and night
it is one of the most beautiful places in the city.

The Neglected Dog Down the Street

Even the street light
out on the corner
seemed to be dim
in front of the house
where the old dog lives.

The rusted fence gate
haphazardly hangs
from a busted hinge
behind the house
where the old dog lives.

There is an old woman
in a dingy sun dress
with a heart aching story
inside of the house
where the old dog lives.

There is a thick air
of long held regrets
and long gone chance
around the house
where the old dog lives.

Lénay
Lénay

She's in touch with
The spirit of the universe

Lénay
Lénay

I'd like to get some
Of that magic of hers

Lénay
Lénay

She's the daughter of the Moon
The Voice of the Wind
The Fay of the Forests
Are all her friends

Lénay
Lénay

She calls the dragons from the Earth
And the Stars down from the Sky.
The secrets of the Soul
Are found within her eyes

Lénay
Lénay

Immortals bow before her
And demons sing her praise
Her laugh will crumble mountains
Her sadness ends our days

Her love is a glorious fountain
Her beauty is the sun's rays
I swear to be her Champion
Idols to her I will raise

Lénay
Lénay

In a dead city
On a long doomed planet
Circling a dying star
There is a shrine erected
By a race strange and bizarre
A shrine to the queen
Of everything; Peace Love and War
And the name of that queen
That pure loving being
Now, then and before

Lénay
Lénay

At the bottom of the ocean
The mermaids sing her name
In the deepest darkest caves
The goblins keep her flame
In the valley of the Centaur Chiefs
They celebrate her fame

Lénay
Lénay
Lénay

At the dawning of Creation
Her Story was set in motion
As an act of elation
And a showing of devotion
The Creators built up nations
And put leviathans in the ocean.
And should it she spurn
Then it will all be burned
And to nothing returned

Lénay
Lénay
Lénay

Sunday Service Is of Little Service to Me

In the back of the hall, I sit with a heart
that rages with vice and boredom
watching the well intended puppet show
all sound and fury signifying community.

But my siren savior, my angel of the morning,
my Highest of the High, Greatest of the Great,
my Sweet Bread of Life, Partner, friend and wife,
is kept away by unavoidable scheduling conflicts.

No number of ivory smiles and gaudy platitudes,
not the greetings of kind eyed strangers,
save my soul from the downward spiral of apathy
or ease my aching heart.

The Gospel of Your Pussy

I thought about you today
and then you surprised me
by just appearing at the glass.
I saw you standing outside
the office looking inside
and I wanted you by my side.
I wanted to get in you
in your mind, in your heart,
your body, right up in your heart
shaped ass where my face
is a perfect fit.
I want to leave teeth marks
where you sit.
I want put my hands
everywhere that you
keep hidden under that
black dress which is,
by the way, one of my favorites.
It's been a long day
but I want to lick you clean
and dirty again.
So you got to shower again.
It ain't in the bible, but it ain't no sin.
but you can get way down
on your knees to pray, anyway.
Pray that we do it again,
and again.
Until the heavenly chorus
gets off watching us
and all the angels gather round
to jerk it to the show and they have
locked the gates of heaven
because nobody's watching the roost,
and Satan gets the Hide-a-key

that nobody thought to move
when he left.
So he walks on in
and sits on the thrown
and calls it home.
From there he shouts that
our love is the purest
and most virtuous
by proclamation of
the New King of Heaven.
That's what I thought of
when I thought about you today.

The Fighters

Their flaws belonged to them
and they had chosen to erect a monument
to their relationship
with its traces of purpled bruises,
badges of a fight well met,
rather than write an elegy.
They are no smashed rebellion
but an ongoing cause to believe in.

Expensive, Lampshade, Bruising, Convincing

Convincing yourself
that the bruising is not
too noticeable
and that you
didn't really like
that lampshade anyway
and that the divorce process
Is lengthy and expensive
and is not what you
really want,
is easier than facing
the truth.

Some of the skills
you have picked up
along the way include
(but are not limited to)
creative use of eyeshadow,
making yourself small
and unnoticeable,
and working quietly
without complaint through
unpleasant circumstances.
It's quite a resume
You have put together.

The Lady and her Fool

As the Lady and her Fool
walked through the garden
they came upon a daffodil lone and golden.
In bunches they can mean great wealth
but in the singular they are a tiding of misfortune.
The Lady's eyes went glassy, her skin fell pale
her manner turned somber and her spirit see-through.
The Fool simply collected the flower
and suggested that their stroll continue.
Along the way they met four wicked and vile children.
So bad were they that you might think Satan bore them.
One of the children asked, "Is that a lone daffodil, harbinger of misery?"
To which the fool replied, "No, child, it is but the first of many."

When my life is at its best
my Mind is not around
to enjoy it.

Instead it is off circling
looking at the lives
of others.

The Admiration of an Anthophile

You ask why I want you
and the answer is difficult
like you can be sometimes
but not impossible.
So I will try.

The majestic agave blooms
so infrequently and irregularly
that predicting the flowering
can be impossible.
but it is worth the wait.

Producing thirty foot stalks
of bright warm yellow
flowers that paint
the remote stone desert
but it is worth the trip.

Your blooming beauty
is much more regular
and produces a much
warmer and richer hue.
So I will hold space.

When your flower
is out of season,
still, you provide shade
to the burdened
So I love you.

I am not a gardener
trying to prod your growth
and you are not a plant

to be maintained or trained.
So I love you.

When ol' Sysifus finally
learns to just relax
and forgives himself
and just enjoys watching
that great rock roll down,
he'll feel life turn around.

I
fawn over you
fall down for you,
fuck up with you,
freak out about you,
fight against you,
flinch away from you,
flake on you,
float behind you,
flounder beneath you,
and
flourish beside you.

A spirit trapped
in the depths of me
standing chest deep
in stagnant emotion
fouled by apathy
fought to escape.
Chewing like a rat
the spirit tore a hole
through my heart box
to let the breath flow
and with it the past
was let go.

I seek asylum in your heart box.
The place where in desperation
the sculptor snapped and made
a stone cell with no entrances
or exits, no widows, nor views.

Just you inside bouncing
off the walls.

Me outside pacing like
a caged wolf.

Those walls are fated
to crumble
whether it is you
or I
or time that decides
is unsure.

Frustration

The one was a dog
who wouldn't come
in from the snow,
as the other stood
holding the door
letting in the cold

The Coming Spring

When thaws the ice
and the cold is spent,
the Sun shall rise
from winter's crypt
and release all lives
from oblivion's grip.
The world will thrive
to spite Hades trick.

Then, snakes will writhe
and the honey drip.
The birds will fly
on northbound trips.
Prey bare new life
Beasts take the scent.
The wild hunt or die.
None stay innocent.

Wind like vernal sighs
will bring lover's gifts
with yearning eyes
and eager lips,
welcoming thighs
and stiffened pricks,
Pants, moans, and cries
signal Spring's ascent.

Spring's Supplicant

Spring's warm scissors
shear my winter shroud.
I shed my covering.
I feel desiccated.
I am face fasted,
deprived of light.

The sun, that buck
of the sky,
Thrusts away the
gray with antlers
that shine.

The sun sprays.
I drink it in.
I swallow it up.
It is on my skin
entering me, filling me.

I spread myself
I submit.
I unfurl. I let go
of myself.
I bloom.

Of all those who would rather
dance in the lights of dreams
than struggle in reality's shade,
I ask only that you call for me
to join the next time you leave.

CBGB

The walls going down
the back stairwell were
smooth white plaster
that stands out still
perfect in some parts.
Some dreamer kid
trying to start a band
put up a sign.
A sketchy tweeker
came along with
another sign
trying to sell an amp.
A girl with violet hair
wrote a poem in sharpie
and an activist tried
to make the world
better with a bumper sticker.
Band names, coin machine stickers,
yard sales, help wanted
and rude jokes.
Repeat, ad infinitum.

If you can get past
the disorganized beauty
of the stairwell walls
and down into shop,
you'll meet a girl
if you're lucky.
She is smart enough
to be funny
and funny enough
to seem ridiculous
and you won't believe

she is talking to you.
A woman with beauty
matched only by
her ability to rip
herself apart
in the cruelest ways.

If you get a chance
tell a joke.
Do whatever it takes
to get a laugh.
Making her smile
is the completely
selfish act of some
greedy bastard
who wants to
feel fucking good
about himself
if only for bit.
Totally worth it.
Because, get this,
if you can make
her crack a smile
though she will try
to hide it from you,
the high you get
is un-god-damn-believable.

Every Direction

As we two walked
down the street
thousands of birds
screeching disorderly
lit from the trees
into the murky sky
She pointed and said,
"That's me."
I asked, "Which one?"
and she said,
"All of them."

Deluge

You stood in the rain on dreamy streets
and I offered to take you somewhere
The rain came down in wicked sheets
and when it ended early that day
we parted. I went carried out my own way
but I caught memories of you.
Your scent clung on the warming breeze
Again, and again, I felt you.
You were on the air.

Meet Cute

I was stuck at the corner
at a cliché crossroads.
Waiting for the light to go.
You were coming out
of the bookstore
hauling a an armload
of feminist socialist guides.
I hung out the window
shouting my stupid love
like a madman, like a fool.
I saw it too in your face.
For a moment we were
that moment
that time in the rom-com
where the button down guy
falls for the wild woman.
Then the light went green
and I left.

END SCENE

Love Languages

On the longest and darkest night
I marched to Babylon by candlelight.
I met a traveler who joined my side
and asked me questions to pass time.

Are you going to enjoy the view?
No, there is a girl that love's me true.
Do you think she will remember you?
To the heavens, I pray she do.

Then we saw the tower smokin'
and knew God's wrath had been awoken
We heard the people's words all broken.
His hate and vengeance was set to motion.

I searched for the girl who had loved me so.
I found her safe from God's angry blow
and my eyes with sadness did overflow.
For now, she loved in ways I couldn't know.

Inside

I dance across the rooftops
of the skyline of my mind.
unbalanced but unfrightened.
Daring to reveal so much. It is printed on
the eyes I watch you with. I am happily
embarrassed my unguarded foolishness,
but unashamed for my enthusiasm.

Outside

I stumble over the order
of my mischosen words
and I question my placement, my posture,
my positioning, my presence, my preoccupation.
I am a fool, a flagellant, who lashes himself
over every misstep whether misperceived
or otherwise.

Like a Hole in the Head

I was skeptical at best
when she first came to me
expounding the benefits
of self-trepanation.
The increased blood flow,
the oxygenation, the euphoria,
the express ticket to enlightenment.

Nothing else had worked though
and it seems to work for other folks.
So I did a little research
had a couple consultations,
shopped the job around.
I finally found someone
to do a little pin hole
and it was kinda nice.
My baby got one too.
It was pretty smooth.

Then shit I thought
I should step it up a notch
to double ought.
Why the fuck not?
Let the love of
the whole entire fuckin' universe
and all the inhabitants in.
I found this far out broad
with a boutique shop downtown
who could get that hole punched.
And it was good.

What they don't tell you
(or maybe I wasn't listening)

is how that hole effects the
people around you,
jealousy and insecurity
and the questioning of
what's so great about the hole
or how much effort
you got to put into that hole
brush your teeth, trim the nose,
swab the ears, and treat the hole.
If you just let it ride
infection gets inside.

It turned out, I guess,
not to be for me.
I tried at least.
I mean I put my skull
(read as heart)
on the line.
Made myself open, vulnerable.
That should count for something.

Anyways,
I got the hole plugged.
That same broad
was kind enough to help
and life is good now,
different but good, better in fact,
than life previous to the hole.
But shit if sometimes, just sometimes,
I don't miss that goddamned hole.

Shitty Angsty Poem

If you were my girl
I would fuck it up
If you let me in your world
I will fuck it up

At first it might be ok
you might say geat.
Because, hey we're
both getting laid
and the weed
is pretty ok.

But I only have
three moods
and two are just
shitty attitudes
and the other
is just being
overly attached
to you.
It's only a matter
of time
before I
say something
rude.

Your friends
will hate me
and ask why
you date me.
But we'll have fun
until we don't
and then we won't

when all that's left
is a bag of stems and seeds
and the stains and scars
of our misdeeds
and you will be happy
to see me leave.

So be my girl
Let me fuck it up.
Let me in your world.
Let's fuck it up.

Top of the Heap

I was the last of them.
When everyone else
was getting love right,
I was the last
and greatest screw up.
Even when losing
was out of style.
I made a real art of it.
I could nose dive
a passionate romance
just... like... that.
When other people zigged,
not me baby.
I rushed straight into
brick walls at top speed
with my heart
dragging by a chain
hooked to the rear bumper.
Sure there used to be others,
but none quite so
devastatingly adept
at disaster as me.
I had a method, see,
a real technique.
I'd find me someone
who is earnest and honest
and who cut out the bull.
Then I'd build up a story
all in my noggin,
In every word or move
I'd find a hidden motive,
an agenda behind the truth.
Then WHAMO BABY!

Here come the flames
right into ashes.
No more love.

Weathering the Storm

Dark clouds hung over the sea
for greater than a week.
Signs were plenty to see.
The creatures took note
Birds silenced their throats
and the bugs burrowed
down to the earth below.
Even the old dogs moaned.
The dawn's red sky boiled
and cold winds had blown
But no one called the ships back home.

When the first thunder clap sounded,
so faint and distant,
it might've been just a gust
and iff'n you blink you'll have miss it.
Just a seasonal cloudburst
or a local disturbance
with a chance of blowing past?
So no one called the ships back home.

The town bundled up against the cold
sealing the shutters, raising their collars
and then rushing past each other
to get their business done and over.
Young men and women turned
their faces away from the rain
Elder folks wrung their hands in pain.
But no one called the ships back home.

Lightening touched and scorched
the old harbor bunkhouse,
the flames burned the boarders out.

Lamp oil fueled fires spread
like unspoken creeping dread
across the rain soaked docks
and the charred remains fell
to the rocks in the roiling sea below.
But no one called the ships back home.

When finally the tour had run its course
and by schedule, not by force
the fleet made its way ashore.
The crews were soaked,
the sails were torn
and timbers broken.
But the air was light
and no eulogies spoken.
The sailors carried a song
and the nets were full.
Neither at sea nor ashore
had a life been lost
Time and worry
were the only lasting costs.
No one into the sea was tossed.
The rains dried, buildings were mended.
And though the town was changed
when the storm had ended,
they were all the richer
for having lived it.

Odysseus's Nostalgia
for the Siren's Song

Frayed bits of cotton
protected my crew
from the Sirens' song,
but I was launched into lust
by those seductive chords
even over the ocean's roar.
It stuck with me, in me,
and pulled me.
Even after returning home
and seeing my life in chaos
and the neglect of Argos,
I thought of those calls
to abandon fondly.
As I cleared the halls
of rotten suitors,
and after that
went about fixing
the damages I brought
to Penelope,
partner of my spirt,
I felt a yearning
for the certain oblivion
and sweet stinging comfort
found in that Siren's call.

Prometheus Makes Excuses

My brother says, "The road to hell
is paved with good intentions."
But that's just the kind of
judgmental post game
armchair commentary
I don't need
and I'm not asking for.

I always try to just
keep looking ahead
and, it seems,
at least to me anyways,
that the road to hell
isn't paved at all.
In some spots,
it's damn rough rock
that will hang you up
for an entire day
while the bird circles
waiting for you to drop
and in other places along the way
it's wet, boggy, unformed clay
that someone with the right
frame of mind might use
in an interesting way.

I was only making up for my brother's
chronic short sightedness.
Yeah sure I wanted people
to like me, maybe even,
love me.
What's so wrong with that?
And yeah, I gave some

of what wasn't mine to give,
but I expected so little
in return.

Maybe that was always
my downfall.
Always loving
the things I make
and wanting others
to love them too.
Sure it's been hard on me.
My lifestyle that is,
and the doctor says
all this stress
is murder on my liver.

Relatable

How many trips to Home Depot
did it take for poor Daedalus
to complete the Labyrinth?
Did he measure twice and cut once
or like me did he rush in
without a care for aesthetics
in favor of practicality?
Eventually sacrificing even
function to just finish the job.

Did Odin question the motives
of Huginn and Muninn whose flights
brought to him daily news of Midgard?
Were the biases of those devine birds
as evident as our modern creature preachers
the fox and the peacock?
Did Ratatösk feed fake news
among the branches and roots
of that rotting tree, Yggdrasil?

Would the Samaritan have stopped
to help that man along the road
if everyday he saw the same man
dressed in different clothing?
If the traveler had a funny sign
would he have been more
or less likely to give aide?

Locked

For those who seek only triumph
and shun life's other pleasures,
those who see each encounter as a battle
calling for the last full measure
and for who compromise
is commensurate to failure,
your prize is hidden and obscured
in a chasm that divides you from others.

In the dusty bed of a long gone river
the resting place of obstinate warriors,
two rams who fought for the pass.
Their bleached bones lie together.
Their horns still locked
marking the spot
where they both fell
where they both failed.
Their fate is your only treasure

Simple Life

Seated deep in isolation
hidden in rows of corn
is a gaunt idiot fellow
with a gap tooth grin.
He doesn't know of the world
except as he is told
and that it's a bowl of sin.
Those dry stalks rise around him
like the masts and riggings of ships
on a dazzling sea of dirt.
The ships travel nowhere
and bring news of the nothing.
He knows in no uncertain terms
that his relatives were right
and that beyond those fields
is a wicked parade of evils
lead by blue hooved devils.
So he would live his life
seated deep in isolation.

The Theorists' Invocation to the Muse

Bring to me updates! Notify me and share news
of man's social anxieties, and the fear
of the world from which constant omens
of death are broadcast, and all our woes
and all our ill-conceived emoji filled statuses
are fed to our groups, circles, friends, and followers.

Chorus:
Fake News! Fake News! Fake News!

Retweet! @Heav'nly Muse,
that in the backrooms of pizza parlors of D.C.
or hidden within Hollywood studio offices
the children of America are spoilt
at the will of the reptile lords.
Those malcontents of the shifting forms
Who farm our misery and madness
To fuel journeys to far flung planets.

Chorus:
Fake News! Fake News! Fake News!

Wrote in the mysts of Illuminatus
across the heavens in the trails
of the fiery winged chariots driven by
faceless agents of the new world order
are tales of plague, pox, disease and disorder.
Their plans concocted to make warriors
of men like Lee Harvey and Ruby and Sirhan
and Ray and Kaczynski and Chapman
and to control men's minds and push forward
Wars over imaginary lines called borders.

Chorus:
Fake News! Fake News! Fake News!

Godcast out across the lines your words,
ye bards of truth. Post upon the boards
the darkened and denied facts of a flat world,
the plans of the phycian and apothecaries
to inject your young with illnesses' seed.
Forward the wisdom of prophets
of doom and damnation and epithets.
Guide my mind and hands as I craft
my monthly manifesto and newsletter.

The Dreamer's Prayer

Now I lay me down to fly
through the fog of cold dark night.
I pray the lords my soul to find
somewhere within my resting mind
where I dip my toes in the river Styx
and hold my breath through the witch's bridge.
I'll salute the legions of ghostly listeners
and be seduced by three weird sisters.
The paint will peel from my wooden feet
and then I'll spit out some rotten teeth.
I'll sneak right past the maiden with no face
whose toothy mouth is on her waist,
and if there's time I'll pay the fee
for the gypsy to sing to me
how my soul can be freed
from inside the crooked steeple
down the lanes of cold dead people.

But if I wake before I find that place
let tomorrow pass with haste
so that I might return there soon
to the land behind the moon.
Please, oh lords, do grant this boon,
but if my request you do refuse,
and your kin do rightly choose
to keep my aching misplaced soul,
I pray it be oh not over bold
if I ask that you can keep it whole.
I beg you please to safely keep it
for I am told that I do dearly need it
to repay those in life that I have cheated
and there's a part of me that does believe it.

Dark Follower

Cast there on the floor
between myself and the door
blocking the path of egress
out of my bleak cramped office
my shadow lies upon his back
poised and ready for attack
against myself, his rightful master.
It is deserved vengeance he is after
for the time I've wasted in the glow
of the harsh fluorescent yellow
and an existence on the tiles
of retail store's doldrum aisles.
Rather he had trailed and mirrored
a man respected and revered.
Had he been projected by the light
shown upon some adventuring kind,
had he stretched across the sands
of far distant and wondrous lands,
he may not spend so much time
with violent murder on his mind,
but following a poor working joe
has worn him thin, mad, and hollow.
So he disappears at night
dreading the summoning of the light
and in the corners he does weep
just passing time between my sleeps.
When his empty weakness is overcame
then my lifeblood he will rise to claim.
He threatens daily to take my place
and become a shadow with my face.

Jack seeks and Audience with the King of Sleep

Rah Rah, King of Sleep,
Do ya think me a fool?
No son, no Jack
only the Lord's tool.
You struggle for a penny.
You toil in disdain.
You work your life away
In your master's name.

Jack be free.
Jack it's known.
Jack your life,
it is your own.

Bah, bah, King of Sleep,
Ya do take me for a fool.
Ya do sir, aye sir.
Ya be mighty cruel.
I strive ta get ta heaven
and ta clear my sins.
The Lord's man on Sunday
says that's how ya do get in.

Jack be free
Jack It's known.
Jack your life,
it is your own.

Rah, Rah, King of Sleep
Mayhap you do speak true
Yes son, yes Jack
I want the best for you,
mercy for your body

and your mortal soul
and mercy for your mind
so your spirit may be whole.

For I will consider Sleep

For She takes the others away so that I am
alone with my thoughts and she is my only
thought.

For when I turn to her for solace and respite
She is nowhere to be found, and She comes
to me instead on her own schedule not
concerning herself with my needs.

For She knows Her prowess as a silky
seductress and will take me into her world
on Her own terms.

For my desire for Her outweighs Her need
of me, as I am only one humble subject in
Her kingdom filled with waiting suitors.

For every night I am without Her, I am
measurably that much worse and the decay
is visible on my spirit and form.

For though She takes me into death,
She revives my mind, body, and soul only so that
I might return to Her again.

For Her I count the moments, and perform
arcane mathematics to calculate how much
time I will have with Her when I am united
with Her... If I am united with Her.

For Her I ritualistically prepare myself and
prepare a place in my home so that She will
come more willing to me.

For having gone without Her I know that I will never make it should my being continue forward in this way.

For She is the end goal of my every day.

For Sleep is who allows me to dream.

The Black Market of the Mind

Fleeing from the bustle
and the shouting of the bazaar
down one of the city's many
seedy side passages
lined with leaning Berber tents
I met a man known as
the memory merchant
pushing his esoteric wares
from behind a thick cover of canvas.
Within the swarthy dealers shop
the air was heavy and flush
with a cacophony of thoughts,
a full stock of exotic sentiments.
The lilac smell of grief,
the citric tang of serenity,
and the woody air of disbelief
swirling all around me.
On his main table was nice
but humdrum stuff
first kisses, last days of summer,
nightmares, mostly fluff.

He saw how I was unimpressed
and gave a sly wink and nudge.
He looked to see that all was clear,
and offered to show the rest.
From beneath a table
of petty grievances aged and old
he pulled a delicate case
that had a gleam like gold
Within his illicit box
were rare and smuggled
much sought after thoughts

like the regret of missed opportunities
and the joy of canceled plans,
the rage one harbors towards one's self
and submission to life's demands.
He had a vial of the ecstasy
of fantasies realized
and a sachet of color me surprised.
There was contempt for authority
and the blind trust of a child,
some acceptance of mortality,
and terror harvested in the wild.

I sampled some mild annoyances,
arousal, and anticipation,
and I left the tent with a fresh supply
of sympathy, satisfaction, and elation.

Design No. 47 "ACME"

Lunar thought cops
sit nodding in satisfaction
in dimly lit tea houses
sipping oolong from
delicate porcelain.

The way out kids
trade the outlines
of daydream aching
interior monologues
for amazing stax of dollars.

While average schlub
worker bees petition
for more law and order
and more agreeable news
beamed to their video screens.

The men in the tower
rub their greasy greedy palms
as everything is going to plan.
Their portfolios are up
and no one asks questions.

Bring Me Stephen Tobolowsky

We need a work horse,
a natural, never seems forced,
who can play up the dweeb,
and make our weak lead
look as cool as a pack of smokes
rolled in a greaser's sleeve.

A guy that's on time
and knows his lines.
He hits his marks.
Makes the total best
of every small part.
Playing the square
for him is a fine art.

Give me a spineless
sniveling perv,
like a beaten cur.
Give me a villain
a smug bureaucrat
maliciously compliant.

He's our timid John,
our targeted mark
for the long con,
our nuisance, our gall midge,
our smirking son of a bitch.
our stoolie, our snitch.

Bring Me Stephen Tobolowsky

Dog Eat Dog

When people complain that the world is insane
and that each new generation fails
to new depths of degradation
or how things were better before
and cities aren't safe spaces no more
I think about how rarely it seems
that one human feasts
on the flesh of another human being
so uncommon it is, in fact,
when someone does commit the act
it becomes sensational national news
generating millions upon millions of views.
So when you feel down
about the world all around
remember to keep the perspective
people in general as a collective
agree that cannibalism is bad.

I walked to County
to see my baby on a slab.
Walked through the pouring rain
No money for a cab.
When I finally arrived
I couldn't get inside.
This time is for family
not my worthless hide

Went to the parlor
to see her there
all painted up
face nails and hair
still saw the rope burns
from the last time she tried
never left a not
no reasons why

Funeral Planning

The hollering produced by my burial
should be heard from here to Olympia.
Everyone will have their assignments.
I need to be tidied up for the show
and then dumped into the ground
below a driftwood cross. Even though,
you know how I would feel
about that kind of thing.

My friend, Robert Nixon,
who I haven't met yet,
but there's still time,
will tell the potato story,
the one about smoking
inferior weed in the desert
out of a hollowed out spud
and then misquote me
several times.
Also, Bobby can misattribute
to me some shit Tony said.
It won't matter much.
Because, you know? We're dead.

Some late comers will roll in
some sleeper friends
who no one knew would come.
One of them will drunkenly
demand everyone laugh and celebrate,
because that's what I would have wanted,
but it's not. It's all right here.
I'm leaving nothing to chance.

My girl, maybe 2 girls,
or a whole processional of girls

of every race, creed, and color,
will take crying to new heights
and then everyone stands silent
and vacant like new orphans
kicked into the system
waiting for the nice lady
from social services
to tell them everything is ok and
point them where to lay down.

illustration of author by
artist Marc Hert

Jonathan S Baker lives in southern Indiana with his gorgeous partner Lénay and his dog. He pays the bills by spreading the word around town in a little white truck.

CPSIA information can be obtained
at www.ICGtesting.com
Printed in the USA
FSHW011955140819
61067FS